My Journal!

Hi! This is your own personal journal! It is a book where you record your own special feelings, thoughts, and experiences.

You can write about anything you wish. You may want to write about your friends and family or you may wish to describe your feelings about a special event. You are free to write about anything you choose no matter how important or unimportant it may seem.

Keep your journal handy where you can write in it often. When you complete your journal, keep it in a safe place. You will enjoy reading it many times in the years ahead.

Tips for writing in your journal:

1. Write about whatever you want. Feel free to express your feelings and emotions.
2. Don't worry about punctuation or spelling mistakes. You can always make the corrections after you've written in your journal.
3. There is no right or wrong way to write in your journal. Just write!

Some Journal Topics

I'm So Brilliant!
If I Could Choose My Family
The Person I Most Admire
My Best Talent
My Most Fearful Thoughts
My Favorite Book
If I Were Teacher for a Day
Why Follow the Rules?
My Best Idea
Honesty is the Best Policy
Save for a Rainy Day
My Homework Excuse
I Like Me!
If I Were Famous….
My Message to the World
The Thing I Most Worry About

My Favorite Place to Visit
A Tough Decision
My Favorite Music
My Most Embarrassing Moment
A Birthday to Remember
My Dreams for the Future
The Best Parents
If I Had a Million Dollars!
My Greatest Accomplishment
Friend or Foe
I'm Feeling "Blue"
My Very Best Friend
It's Better to be….
When I Grow Up….
Three Wishes
Stand Up for What You Believe

Date

Date _____

Date _____

Date

Date _____

Date _____

Date

Date

Date _____

Date _____

Date _____

Date

Date _____

Date _____

Date

Date _____

Date

Date

Date _____

Date _____

Date

Date _____

Date _____

Date _____

Date

Date _____

Date

Date _____

Date

Date _____